PROPHETIC COACH MANUAL

DAN MCCOLLAM

PROPHETICCOMPANY.COM

TABLE OF CONTENTS

INTRODUCTION

More than a decade ago, a wise prophet asked me, "Are we a prophetic company or do we just love prophecy?" At that time, I didn't know what a prophetic company was, much less how or why I would want to build one. Today, I celebrate the fact that the term "prophetic company" is coming into popular use all over the world. Though the phrase can mean different things to different people, prophetic people and purposes are healthiest in the safety of a loving, accountable prophetic community.

In my earlier book entitled *Prophetic Company*, I go through an introduction to the biblical concept, the history, and the emergence of our own prophetic community into a five-spoke model that includes team members, coaches, mystics, prophets, and presbyters. This five-spoke structure forms a prototype wine skin that is important to the development of healthy, well-balanced prophetic communities. The purpose of this book is not to rehash those concepts but to zero in on the coach spoke and lay out the values, the purpose, the skill sets, and the responsibilities of a local prophetic team coach along with some practical tips and protocols for building and strengthening a prophetic team. This book can serve as both a recruiting and a training tool in the hands of any potential or current coach. Prophetic coaches serve as a vital key to building effective teams and strengthening a prophetic community.

Throughout this manual, I will be speaking to you as if you were one of the coaches in my own prophetic community. While everything contained within is subject to your community's own interpretation and culture in the practical application of it, I will use a tone that implies more than casual suggestion. These principles are what I would do in my community, and for the purposes of this book, you are part of my community.

CHAPTER 1
CHANGING LIVES

W hy be a coach? Prophetic ministry changes lives. Look at the following example of how prophetic ministry helped transform an ordinary guy into the first ruling king of his nation.

> *After that you will go to Gibeah of God, where there is a Philistine outpost. As you approach the town, you will meet a procession of prophets coming down from the high place with lyres, timbrels, pipes and harps being played before them, and they will be prophesying. The Spirit of the LORD will come powerfully upon you, and you will prophesy with them; and you will be changed into a different person.*

> *1 SAMUEL 10:5-6*

In these verses, the prophet Samuel promises a budding young Israeli king that by simply entering into the atmosphere of prophetic ministry he would be transformed into a different person. I have personally witnessed this happen; I have seen lives changed as a result of prophetic ministry.

Personally, the prophetic words I have received over the years have significantly shaped and shifted the person I am today. Prophetic ministry calls out our heavenly identity, establishes destiny, speaks to blind spots of potential assignments, and confirms areas of gifting and calling. Prophecy releases new things, fresh graces, and initiates new seasons in our lives.

I remember the first time I saw prophetic ministry in action. I was raised in a wonderful, loving, evangelical home, but we were definitely a "non-prophet organization." At 23 years old, my wife Regina and I were invited to serve as the vocational youth pastors at a fiery revival church in the grassy hillsides of Northern Kentucky. At this new church, prophetic words were the norm. One Sunday evening a prophet was a guest speaker at our church. I was absolutely fascinated that someone could hear from God so clearly and profoundly. As he called out specific individuals for prophetic ministry, I observed the impact it released on people's lives, not to mention how deeply the prophetic words we received affected Regina and me. In that moment, I knew that prophetic ministry was something I wanted to be a part of for the rest of my life. I understood that prophetic ministry possesses the power to transform lives.

Coaching a prophetic team is your opportunity to be an essential part of this life-changing ministry. Some of our greatest Bible heroes like Abraham, Sarah, Moses, David, Deborah, and Apostle Paul were all transformed or shaped through prophetic encounters. World-changers are made in an atmosphere of God-encounters, and prophetic ministry offers the opportunity for one of those defining moments to uncover God's greater purposes for our lives. Understanding the importance of prophetic ministry, let's look for a moment at the goals of a prophetic team.

THE LOVE KEY

Love stands as the most monumental purpose and fundamental goal of prophetic ministry. Someone should feel seen, known, and loved through a prophetic exchange. The Bible explains that if we can fathom jaw-dropping mysteries and speak profound prophetic words laced with incredibly accurate words of knowledge but do not have love, we are nothing. (1 Corinthians 13:2) Any prophetic mastery apart from love is vacant and hollow. Accuracy without affection is ultimately ineffective.

Love is the single most transforming force in the universe. The apostle Paul wrote to the Galatian church, *"The only thing that counts is faith expressing itself through love." (Galatians 5:6b)* This Scripture makes it evident that all acts of faith not motivated by love do not count. This is consistent with the teaching of Jesus. We know that Jesus and the early Church fathers taught that the entire law is fulfilled in keeping this one command: *"Love God and love your neighbor as yourself." (Mark 12:31-*

33, Luke 10:27, Romans 13:10, Galatians 5:14) In these same verses, we see that everything written in the Law and the Prophets can be fulfilled by love; so, it's not hard to understand that love must be the ultimate goal and protocol for every prophetic exchange. I unfold this concept in detail in my book *Love and Prophecy*. It is mandatory reading for all my coaches and team members.

Love is also the bridge through which supernatural intelligence flows. God's great love is both the access point and the delivery system for prophetic revelation. The great agricultural scientist and inventor, George Washington Carver, said, *"Whatever you love opens its secrets to you."*

This is how I apply this love principle to a prophetic exchange: whenever I feel like I don't have any prophetic revelation for a person, I lean back into the Father's love for them. I allow my heart to warm with the sense of His great love for this person, and the prophetic content begins to bubble-up within me. From that flowing stream of love, I begin to broadcast the wonders of God's heart and mind toward the receiver. Love is the source of supernatural secrets and the primary goal of any successful prophetic coach. Prophetic ministry must be a divine extension of the love of God. With this goal in mind, if a person leaves your prophetic ministry session feeling loved, then you have been a seriously successful coach.

ENCOURAGE, STRENGTHEN, COMFORT

All prophetic team ministry is based upon the foundation laid in Scripture, as no true prophetic word will ever counter God's written word. The three targets of prophecy most clearly and plainly defined in New Testament teaching are the commands to strengthen, encourage, and comfort. (1 Corinthians 14:3) As I have shared in all our Prophetic Company books and training, these three virtues provide more than a warm, fuzzy feeling. They build much more than a bless-me-club culture. These three target virtues catapult a person into their life-changing destiny.

In the Old Testament, whenever a person or group of people were about to take hold of an earth-shaking destiny, they would be given this command, "Be strong and courageous for the Lord your God is with you." In both the Old and New Testaments, strength, courage, and comfort are the graces that transform lives and propel people into their earth-shaking destinies. Can you see the power of our three secret weapons here? Prophetic teams with this target can't help but add value to the people and places around them. A Prophetic Company coach carries a commitment to prioritizing and releasing these three virtues.

TEAM SYNERGY

God poured His Spirit out on all flesh so that every individual can prophesy, but that doesn't mean He wanted us to do it alone. Scripture calls us to be part of a greater vision—a body of believers with various flavors and perspectives who together release the power and love of God in its various forms. The Old Testament prophets were healthiest and happiest when they were gathered in prophetic companies or communities. Likewise, our Lord Jesus sent His disciples out in teams, as did the early Church. Even the Godhead—Father, Son, and Holy Spirit—operates as a team. That is why we build prophetic team ministry.

Coaches use team ministry to harness the power of spiritual synergy. The Oxford Dictionary defines synergy as:

> *The interaction or cooperation of two or more organizations, substances, or other agents to produce a combined effect greater than the sum of their separate effects.*

True synergy within any team creates greater productivity. The impact of prophetic ministry grows exponentially through the healthy contribution of multiple team members. That is why Scripture says, *"Let two or three prophesy and let the rest weigh carefully what is said." (1 Corinthians 14:29)* Why two or three? Because we are so much stronger together. Synergy is not merely adding content (1+1+1=3); it is a multiplied, exponential increase of anointing, depth, and clarity (1+1+1=300).

The apostle Peter speaks of the diversity of each individual contribution, *"Each of you should use whatever gift you have received to serve others, as faithful stewards of God's grace in its various forms." (1 Peters 4:10)* Though I don't agree with or endorse his beliefs, I do like the way the Japanese poet, Ryunosuke Satoro, expressed the concept of synergy in relationships, *"Individually, we are one drop; together, we are an ocean."* Synergy multiplies strength. Alone, our contribution is a significant drink for a thirsty soul; together, we are an ocean of refreshing to the world.

Synergy is not based on conformity or unanimity. In other words, synergy is not simply agreeing on something or replicating something. True synergy is not achieved by everyone doing or saying the same thing but by each one contributing their unique part or sound to a greater symphony. Unity, continuity, and common values are important matters of the heart, but it is our differing gifts, graces, perspectives, and contributions that make team ministry more effective.

An example of team synergy is found in the metaphor of the parts of the human body penned in Paul's writings,

> *If the whole body were an eye, where would the sense of hearing be? If the whole body were an ear, where would the sense of smell be?*

> 1 CORINTHIANS 12:17

Different team members each use their unique spiritual receptors to release a more circumspect, or manifold, wisdom of God over the receiver. Some team members are hearing while others are seeing; some are sensing and others perceiving. In anatomical terms, some of us are the eyes, some are the nose, and some are the ears, etc. Our contributions, which are coming from different perspectives, multiply the accuracy and strength of the whole. Coaches build the synergy by facilitating the partnership and contribution of each part of the body. I will explain later in this manual exactly how; for now it is enough to see the goal and target of the concept.

So why would someone choose to coach a prophetic team? Let's recap the main ideas of this chapter. Prophecy changes lives. The prophetic atmosphere you radiate can turn the heart of a commoner to a king. The words of your team members have the power to encourage, comfort, and strengthen someone into an earth-shaking destiny. Furthermore, your prophetic team possesses the ability to release the most powerful substance in the universe—the love of God! Love brings heaven to earth. And don't forget that the synergy you create by working as a team can be exponentially greater in impact than anything you could ever achieve alone. In these ways, coaches live and serve as world changers.

CHAPTER 2
CHOOSING LEADERS

*"After this the LORD appointed seventy-two others and
sent them two by two ahead of him to every town and place
where he was about to go."*

LUKE 10:2

he business legend Andrew Carnegie said,
*"Teamwork is the fuel that allows common people to
attain uncommon results."* I wrote in the last
chapter that the synergy of prophetic teams changes
lives, but an effective team requires strong leadership.
Coaches are not appointed to limit or police the input of
individuals but to harness the synergistic effects of each
team member's contribution to the whole. In this
chapter, we are going to talk about what it takes to
become a leader of a prophetic team.

PROPHETIC SKILLS

A coach needs four categories of basic skills to be successful with the team: prophetic, people, organizational, and character skills. The first is obvious. To be a prophetic coach you need to be skilled at giving prophetic words. Now, before you disqualify yourself as "not that prophetic," you should know that you don't have to be the best or most accurate prophetic voice on your team. A prophetic coach needs to be solid and comfortable stirring up the gift of prophecy (2 Timothy 1:6), but they don't have to be the best at prophesying.

Plainly stated, a coach must be comfortable enough prophesying to ensure that every client hears at least one accurate and actionable word wrapped in the love of God. Oftentimes, your team members will together deliver strong content that is just what the receiver needs. However, if your team members speak a lot of sweet and affirming spice but no real actionable depth, it is your job to "bring the beef." In other words, coaches need to always be ready to share a prophetic word with substance and content so that the receiver benefits from the exchange.

I'm not saying a coach must be the team's prophetic superstar; they should, however, be the most dependable player. Actually, a coach should not be the star of the team. As a coach, I encourage you to seek out at least one team member whom you would consider more prophetically gifted than yourself. This person might be defined as "raw prophetic talent." This person may not be as knowledgeable or refined as you in spiritual matters, but they have good intuitive substance to their words. It often appears that prophetic perceptions come easily to them, and their words receive positive feedback. There are many great reasons to have someone like this on your prophetic team.

One of the greatest growth experiences you will ever know is coaching people with a higher level of gifting or grace than yourself. You will learn so much from one another in a process we call "strategic life-exchange." Great leaders are never intimidated by strong gifting. If leaders allow themselves to be threatened by gifting, they will always keep weak people around them. True leaders know they are appointed by God, not just chosen for their level of gifts. The authority of a true spiritual leader comes from heaven through man and is not based on earthly performance alone. This understanding gives a coach the confidence and security to lead people with gifts greater than their own. When you're not threatened by the gifts of others, you can truly value and appreciate gifted people. Healthy coaches know that their team member's ability to speak a helpful timely word takes pressure off them as a leader. They get to share the load of responsibility while advancing the standard of prophetic accuracy. Prophetic gifting is only one contributing factor in a greater leadership equation.

PEOPLE SKILLS

The second tool a prophetic coach needs for success is people skills. I personally value this one even higher than a person's prophetic abilities. Coaches should be able to gather, connect, and confront people in a healthy way. We will talk more about gathering, connecting, and confronting in later chapters; but a love for people, an ability to communicate, and a desire to see others grow is at the heart of any true Kingdom leader. Great people skills are valuable in any ministry or prophetic work, but for a coach, they make the difference between a prophetic ministry and a prophetic community. A ministry can get the job done, but a community is a culture that cultivates love, friendship, and teamwork. Good people skills strengthen the heart connection between contributing members of a prophetic community. Coaching a prophetic team creates an opportunity to love, build, and connect people within the Body of Christ.

ORGANIZATIONAL SKILLS

Organizational skills are also important for coaches. Calvin Coolidge said, *"The only difference between a mob and a trained army is organization."* A prophetic coach does not need to be a master administrator or organizational genius. However, an effective leader should be able to manage time, make a few calls, and keep their team structure intact. Coaches lead by helping each team member know their role in a prophetic appointment. They assign tasks and appoint who will open and who will close each meeting. Coaches check-in on their team members outside of ministry times to see how they are doing and keep their teams informed of upcoming ministry opportunities in a timely way.

CHARACTER SKILLS

The final quality we look for in a coach is their character skills. People are depending on you, so you must show yourself trustworthy and dependable. Our teams are only as strong as our commitment to the Lord, the community, and our collective goals. Gifting without character undermines the quality and believability of prophetic ministry. Poor character has often given the prophetic a bad name. Coaches are people of character committed to the task of changing lives through prophetic ministry.

COACH COMMITMENTS

An important part of character skills is agreeing to and fulfilling the commitments required of a prophetic coach. Let's look at each of those briefly. First we ask for a commitment to regular coaches' gatherings where we have training and discussions that enable the coach group to grow together as prophetic leaders. Connecting with one another as team leaders builds community and strengthens the bond and focus of our prophetic community.

As mentioned earlier, we also ask coaches to commit to making regular contact with their team members outside of assigned ministry times. Check in with your team regularly just to see how they are doing. Build a heart connection, not just a relationship built around function. If you only call team members when you need something, you might find them dodging your calls. Coaching is a commitment to connection not just function. Our function brings us together, but our friendship binds us together.

Coaches are also asked to assemble their teams for ministry times. This means that when it is time to minister as a team, coaches make the phone calls to inform and gather their members. They make sure that there are an appropriate number of team members ready to minister and to serve for the entire planned ministry time.

Finally, coaches identify and raise up other coaches—they don't just produce, they reproduce. Every healthy tree reproduces after its own kind; coaches should do the same. We ask that coaches be always watching for team members who have leadership potential. Those with leadership potential can be invited to assist the coach in leadership responsibilities. As they grow in leadership, they can be recommended for the coaching position of a new team. We ask coaches to recommend a team member for coach development at least every one to three years.

Coaches are an essential part of advancing and strengthening the prophetic community. The invitation to coach is a recognition of your leadership potential. You are a connector and builder that helps each joint supply what is needed for the whole Body. All of us are growing in skills, so you don't have to be perfect in each of these areas; but these are the basic requirements and qualifications we are looking for in order to be a prophetic team coach.

CHAPTER 3
PROTECTING PEOPLE

"The purpose of my instruction is that all believers would be filled with love that comes from a pure heart, a clear conscience, and genuine faith."

1 TIMOTHY 1:5

Transforming lives through prophetic ministry is also about protecting people. Our goal is to do as much good as possible, but we must also work in such a way as to do as little harm as possible. Most of us have heard stories about people who have been hurt or misguided through prophetic words that lacked proper protocol. One of the coach's chief responsibilities is to know and reinforce the protocols that protect all the parties involved in a prophetic exchange.

A protocol can be defined as *"the official procedure or system of rules governing affairs of state or diplomatic occasions. (Oxford)* Another definition is *"a code prescribing strict adherence to correct etiquette and precedence (as in a diplomatic exchange and in the military services.)" (Merriam-Webster)* Prophetic team members are like ambassadors for the kingdom of God; they are soldiers and commanders who must learn to function within specific guidelines. Protocols provide the etiquette for how we are to conduct ourselves in prophetic ministry. When flowing in the gift of prophecy, we must guard the heart and health of each individual receiver.

When articulating the protocols, we try to keep them short and simple so that every team member can know and memorize them. In short, they are: 1) be encouraging, 2) be responsible, 3) be clear and kind, and 4) be brief and amazing. Every team member should know these four basic protocols by heart, but the coach should understand the reason and root system behind each of these guidelines. In this chapter, I will build out the purpose and biblical basis for each of our prophetic ministry protocols.

BE ENCOURAGING

We already stated in chapter one that every word must encourage, comfort, and strengthen as found in 1 Corinthians 14:3. This Scripture reference is easy to memorize because the verse number (3) corresponds with the number of virtues within this value (3): encourage, comfort, strengthen. The challenge is that not everyone defines these three virtues the same way

—the various interpretations of what someone finds encouraging can be somewhat subjective.

Here is Prophetic Company's first standard for defining encouragement: "If you don't know whether a prophetic word is encouraging or not, then place your hand on your own head and speak it over yourself. If you don't like it, then don't give it to someone else." I know this is simple, and we often say it with a bit of humor, but this description mirrors the law of love that Jesus laid down in Matthew 7:12, *"So in everything, do to others what you would have them do to you, for this sums up the Law and the Prophets."* This verse represents a huge principle. More than four thousand years of Old Testament history could be summed up in loving someone else as you love yourself. Do you see the depth of the root system for this protocol? Love is the source or tap root for encouragement, strength, and comfort as well as the fruit this plant of prophecy should produce.

When speaking of our encouragement protocol, I often hear people say, "But I'm tough. I can take it. I like people to give it to me straight." Usually, what they mean by these types of statements is that they are giving permission for someone to bring correction or rebuke through the prophetic. Since that is the way they think they want to receive truth, they reason it is surely okay to give others those same kinds of harsh or corrective words.

I think we can answer this "tough love view" of prophecy by rooting ourselves in the New Testament's clearly stated difference between the purpose of the prophetic word and the written word of God. The purpose of the written word is defined as follows: *"All Scripture is given by inspiration of God, and is profitable for doctrine, for reproof, for correction, and instruction in righteousness." (2 Timothy 3:16)* The purpose of the prophetic word we have already shared from 1 Corinthians 14:3: *"But the one who prophesies speaks to people for their strengthening, encouraging and comfort."* How much clearer can it get?

In the New Covenant, the written Word (the Bible) is used to establish doctrine, to correct, rebuke, and instruct. We should not use the prophetic word to do what the written word is meant to do—meaning we should not use prophecy to correct and rebuke or define our major doctrines; the Bible provides the source for that. A person can receive prophetic information by the Spirit that they are not supposed to say or act on. Just because a perception is accurate doesn't mean that it is appropriate to share. The proverbs of Solomon tell us that only a fool shares everything they are thinking. We must define encouragement through the filter of love and the wisdom of Scripture.

I have created many resources that go doctrinally deeper into why encouragement is so important in prophetic ministry. For more on this subject get the book *Love and Prophecy*[1] or listen to the audio teaching series called *Living on the Right Side of the Cross*.[2] Coaches guard and protect people by reinforcing the protocol of love and encouragement in all prophetic ministry.

BE RESPONSIBLE

Another safety protocol for prophetic ministry is found in how we handle directional words. Directional words can be defined as those that give specific or implied instructions for a major life decision. These often include prophetic words concerning relationships, employment, difficult life choices, and things like changes in geographical location.

I have heard countless stories of those who have been hurt by words instructing them to marry a certain person, or promising promotions that never came, or predicting babies that were never born. These wrong words have caused some churches and ministries to forbid the use of directional prophetic words at all. In communities imposing directional word limits, prophetic words are used for confirmation and affirmation only. In my opinion, this can be a form of "despising prophecy" or "treating prophecy with contempt" as warned against in 1 Thessalonians 5:20. At Prophetic Company, we believe God wants to direct us through prophetic words, but that God has also set healthy prophetic protocols in place to protect us. Directional words require healthy guidelines on the part of the giver and the receiver in a prophetic exchange.

For the giver of a prophetic word, we encourage each person on a prophetic team to take personal responsibility for the words that they give. Our general principle is: do not give a person a prophetic word that you would not be willing to walk through with them. If you say that there will be a major shift in their life in the next seven days, and that shift does not happen, then you need to process the outcome with that person or apologize and clean-up any damage you caused. Clean-up might include meeting with the person and consulting on how each of you may have misinterpreted or misapplied what was said. It does not mean you always must hash out every detail with every person you give a word to, but maintaining a sense of responsibility will keep your spiritual zeal from getting ahead of your wisdom. Team members should take the prophetic words they are speaking as seriously as the receiver is taking them. Coaches help protect and enforce this healthy sense of responsibility in the team of those giving prophetic words.

For the receiver of a directional word, there is also a responsibility. Receivers have the responsibility to judge and test any prophetic word they receive. One of the ways a team member can keep the receiver aware of their responsibility to judge is to preface a directional prophetic word with some instruction. In my own ministry, if I sense a directional word coming, I often give an exhortation to the receiver that goes something like this, "Now, this next part is more directional, so I am going to ask you to judge it more carefully and throw it out if Holy Spirit does not confirm it to your heart." At Prophetic Company, we reinforce the value that the receiver has the power and responsibility to judge words. (1 Thessalonians 5:19-21, 1 Corinthians 14:29)

Prophetic Company co-founder, Bethany Hicks, says the receiver is more powerful than the giver of a prophetic word. Why would that be true? Because it is agreement that allows a prophetic word to activate in your life. Prophetic words can never be a curse, misleading, controlling, or manipulative if you know your power as a receiver. Nothing can stick to you that you have not come into agreement with. Coaches make sure that givers and receivers of prophetic words are functioning in a healthy and safe protocol of giving and receiving responsibly.

BE CLEAR AND BE KIND

The way you and your team members communicate a prophetic word is also important. Researchers tell us that as little as 7% of our communication is found in the words we speak. The words you say are only one small part of the overall communication process. Up to 55% of communication happens through your body language (your physical position and posture), and around 38% happens through the tone of your voice. Effective communication is so much more than saying the right words. Why is this principle of communication so important to know and understand in prophetic ministry? Because when people are in doubt or have a question about what was communicated, they will interpret the meaning of the word through how it felt, looked, or sounded when delivered.

If you gave someone a great word about being an overcomer but you were making a strange sour face, the receiver might interpret the good things you said as a prophecy of an impending struggle because of the pained look you were making. You never said anything like that with your words, but your facial expression as you were struggling internally to clarify what you were seeing may have communicated trouble. So, the receiver jumps to a wrong conclusion of your word based not upon what you said but upon how you said it. If you talk about boldness but your voice sounds timid, they may not take you or your team member seriously. The word must look, feel, and sound true to the receiver.

Jesus is the master communicator; He was the Word become flesh. (John 1:14) Everything about Him communicated what heaven was saying. Train your team members to communicate with their whole person. Make it your goal in every prophetic exchange to be clear and to be kind.

Focus on clarity. Though prophetic words are sometimes deep spiritual concepts that we are translating into common earthly language (1 Corinthians 2:12-15), you can't allow team members to be overly mystical or ambiguous. Team members often make the mistake of sharing a perception of spiritual information as if it is part of the prophecy itself. For instance, they might say, "I saw you standing in a purple wheat field, the sun was setting, and you were wearing swim fins even though there was no water in sight. I don't know what that means, but that is what I saw." What? Those words are not helpful and certainly not clear. Your perception—the picture you are seeing—

is not the prophecy. A spiritual impression is an invitation to a greater conversation with Holy Spirit. When Jeremiah the prophet's eyes were spiritually drawn to an almond branch, he didn't run around saying, "Almond branch, almond branch. The word of the Lord is almond branch." No, he shared what the almond branch meant, otherwise the message would not have been clear.

It is the team member's responsibility to ask God what is being said through a vision or impression. The vision, impression, sensation, or feeling is not the prophecy, it is the catalyst for the greater conversation. Coaches make sure all prophetic communication is clear. Sometimes clarity for the listener requires asking the question, "Did that mean something to you? Do you resonate with what was said?" If not, we seek to clarify; if everything is clear or meaningful, we move on.

Along with clarity, we are asking team members to be kind. Show the love of God through kindness, humility, and gentleness. Remember that the end result of your prophetic exchange is that the receiver should feel seen, known, and loved by God. The Greek word for "kind" comes from a root meaning "fit for use, virtuous, good, pleasant, manageable." These definitions remind me of a favorite verse from Ephesians 4:29,

> Do not let any unwholesome talk come out of your mouths, but only what is helpful for building others up according to their needs, that it may benefit those who listen.

Try to express your spiritual truths in words and metaphors that would be clear to the receiver. Communicating in this way is a kind thing to do.

Sometimes prophetic people tell me, "Well, I just share whatever God gives me." That sounds spiritual, but the truth is that you share things you have faith to hear and see. Each one will prophesy according to the measure of their own faith. (Romans 12:6) You prophesy the types of things you are used to believing for. Your faith can be adjusted to the needs of your receiver, and so can your language. Jesus could have come to earth talking about black holes in the universe and the laws of quantum physics. He is, after all, the master creator of an exquisitely complex universe. But our Lord didn't do that. He customized His language and His topics to His audience's needs and understanding. To farmers, He presented Kingdom truths as sowing seed; to tax collectors, he shared spiritual truths in terms of money and investments. Jesus used metaphors that spoke uniquely to the life and language of the receiver. This principle and pattern of Christ keeps communication both clear and kind. Coaches help keep all prophetic communication clear and kind by aiming it at the need and language of the receiver.

BE BRIEF AND AMAZING

A prophecy does not have to be long to be powerful. Jesus gave some very short prophetic words that changed people's lives. Sometimes these were a single sentence, like when he said to Nathanael, "I saw you

while you were under the tree." We want team
members to learn how to go deep with prophetic
content quickly and to honor people's time. There are
three basic reasons we put time limits on our prophetic
appointments.

First, we obviously want to serve as many people as
possible. Often our teams will face long lines of
hundreds of hungry hearts waiting for prophetic
ministry. If you take too long with one person, then
someone else might not get their opportunity to receive
a prophetic word. Your team members may ask, "But
isn't it unloving to cut a prophetic word short?" No, it is
maturity. The Bible says, *"The one who has knowledge uses
words with restraint..."* (Proverbs 17:27) Another verse,
found in 1 Corinthians 14:29-31, shares a protocol of
stopping a prophetic word so *"you can all prophesy in
turn so that everyone may be instructed and encouraged."* It
is certainly not kind and loving to keep others waiting a
long time only to deny them their chance to receive
prophetic ministry because your team went too long
with one individual. Team members need to share
briefly so that everyone who wants a word from the
Lord can receive something and be encouraged.

Time limits are also about honoring the receiver's time.
Team members are comfortable and familiar with
prophetic culture and ministry, but not everyone is. It
can be quite overwhelming for someone who is not
accustomed to receiving prophetic words. In this
environment, a little content can go a long way. I have
personally watched the expression on a person's face
move from an intent look of interest to staring off in

space during a prophetic exchange. The receiver at that moment was obviously thinking about the last thing that was said and not listening to what came next. Some receivers start crying the moment the first word is spoken, and it is unlikely that they hear any of the words that follow.

Coaches should pay attention to the receiver and evaluate their capacity in the moment. This is a loving and kind thing to do. Long words can be like eating too much good food. It all tastes great, but you can only digest as much as you have capacity for. If you consume too much, then you feel weighed down. We must be sensitive to people's capacity and not give them too much information. Let's look at the example of Jesus.

Jesus said, *"I have many more things to say to you, but you cannot bear them now." (John 16:12)* Do you see the restraint of Jesus? He only gave people what they were able to receive. Based on this example of Jesus, we teach that love only shares what a person can bear. It's not always loving to share everything that comes to you. Share only what fits in the allotted time frame and what matches the capacity of your receiver.

Time limits are also about giving every team member a turn. The protocol presented to the Corinthian church of Paul's day was this:

> *If a revelation comes to someone who is sitting down, the first speaker should stop. For you can all prophesy in turn so that everyone may be instructed and encouraged. The spirits of prophets are subject to the control of prophets.*

1 CORINTHIANS 14:29-32

I love the way The Message paraphrase puts this:

> *Take your turn, no one person taking over. Then each speaker gets a chance to say something special from God, and you all learn from each other. If you choose to speak, you're also responsible for how and when you speak.*

On prophetic ministry teams, there is often one or two dominant people who, if given the room, will take over. It is the coach's responsibility to make sure every team member gets the chance to share what they receive from God.

I hope you are beginning to see why coaches and our guidelines for prophetic ministry are so important. *"Everything must be done in a fitting and orderly way." (1 Corinthians 14:40)* Protocols protect people from the misuse of prophecy. Our protocols have a strong biblical basis that align with our primary purpose for prophetic ministry. Allowing someone to function outside of these boundaries is dangerous for the receiver and negligent on the part of the coach. Our goal is to build a healthy prophetic community; one of the keys to this goal is coaches understanding and reinforcing healthy protocols.

CHAPTER 4
RECRUITING MEMBERS

"Therefore pray the LORD of the harvest to send out laborers into the harvest."

MATTHEW 9:38

American researcher and consultant Jim Collins said, *"Great vision without great people is irrelevant."* A prophetic community is built through inviting great people to be part of a team. Not everyone is a natural gatherer, but anyone can learn how to recruit people and be successful at it. In this chapter, we will talk about six steps a coach should take to recruit and retain members for their prophetic team.

WATCH

Potential team members are all around you. They are busy people and bored people, skilled people and novices, young and seasoned. The first key to recruiting team members is to open your eyes and look! Watch people and always be looking for your harvest of potential team members. Jesus told his disciples, *"I tell you, open your eyes and look at the fields! They are ripe for harvest." (John 4:35)* Ask the Father to open your eyes to see people who should be part of your team.

Every team is made up of one coach plus a minimum of two to a maximum of five team members. You only need a few members to start an effective team. The long-range goal of a coach should be to recruit more than two team members. By recruiting multiple team members, you can insure that you will have at least two volunteers available each time prophetic ministry opportunities arise.

Start your recruiting journey by writing down a list of people around you who you would like to invite to be part of your team. Look specifically for someone older and someone younger. We love to demonstrate the generations ministering together within a prophetic community. Children and teens can be trained to be effective team members, but make sure to get parental permission before you ask a minor to be part of your team. Often, the parents will join with their child or teen. Your team can fill up quickly that way. Also, look for the treasure of senior citizens. Senior saints often have more available time together with a maturity and wisdom that adds depth to your team's prophetic content.

Remember also to look for someone who you think is more prophetically gifted than you. It's great to have a seasoned team member you can depend on who always seems to have a great word. I also love finding raw and untrained prophetic gifting in a potential team member. Adding them to your team can help them refine their gift into a greater treasure. Many people have a large grace on their gift but not enough wisdom and understanding to make it effective. I feel many churches have a significant number of spiritual people with prophetic gifting but no place for them to serve. You can help give someone the outlet they need for their prophetic perceptions by offering them a ministry opportunity on your team. It's also great to seek out someone who is just starting their prophetic exploration. You will learn a lot about prophetic ministry from working with beginners and novices.

Watch for complimentary players for your team regarding age, skill level, and how they receive information. This contributes to the overall synergy of what your team can deliver in a prophetic appointment. Keep on the watch for new team members even when your team is full, knowing that there is always a natural inflow and outflow of members on any healthy team. Don't assume everyone you recruit will serve with you for the rest of their life. Always keep a watchful eye for potential new members. If your team remains full, you can always refer them to someone else's team that has a need for new members.

PRAY

Before you ask someone to join your team, pray for them and about them. The nineteenth century author and evangelist S.D. Gordan said, *"You can do more than pray after you have prayed but you can never do more than pray until you have prayed."* Recruiting without praying is kind of like trying to plant without plowing. A few seeds might land in a fertile crack or crevice and sprout, but you are decreasing your effectiveness by not plowing the ground first. The same is true in prayer. The Bible says, *"You have not because you ask not."* (James 4:2) In my own life, I am amazed at how many times I have been frustrated with a specific lack of provision only to realize that I had not specifically prayed for that request. I might have complained to God about the problem, but not requested a specific answer. In the same way, I have had coaches who were frustrated about not having enough members on their team when they had failed to pray for new team members. Plow up your fallow ground with prayer.

Praying in advance for the potential recruit has many benefits. First, Jesus commanded that we pray for workers for our harvest field. (Matthew 9:38) Acting on that command is a demonstration of love, faith, and obedience to the Lord. Action with prayer produces more than action by itself. Your prayers prepare the soil of that person's heart to respond. We are not controlling or manipulating other people with our prayer, but we are preparing their hearts to make the best choice for everyone involved. You can pray something like this:

"Father, if this person is a good fit for my team, then I pray You would put a pull on their heart to be part of this prophetic ministry." Also, praying for the person in advance will get them on your mind and heart so that when they do join your team, you will continue in a habit of prayer for that team member.

Prayer also makes sure that you are seeing someone correctly. Talking to God about your potential recruit gives the Holy Spirit an opportunity to fix or improve your vision, especially if there is something greater He wants you to see. Take a few weeks to pray over the names you have put on your potential team members list before moving to the next step. Plow your harvest field with prayer.

INVITE

Did you know that the word "come" is used as an invitation in the Bible more than 1,200 times? Invitation is a huge part of the kingdom of God. Some people are so afraid of rejection that they are hesitant to invite others to be on their team. You need to "flip the script" and change how you think about this matter. Think about the other person—the one you are recruiting. An invitation is an affirmation. It says, "I see you. I want you." People love to be seen and affirmed even if they don't have the time or calling to join your team. It's important to see invitation as a way of demonstrating God's love for people. Sow the affirmation of invitation into your community, and you will reap the benefits of a harvest of workers.

Another key to recruiting is to keep on inviting—not in a nagging way but in healthy persistence. In advertising, there is a principle called the "Rule of 7." It suggests that the average consumer needs to hear a message seven times before they will consider taking action. I don't know all the science behind that, but we all know that repeated messages make a greater impression on us. Sometimes coaches drop a potential team member from their list if they don't get an immediate "yes" to their invitation. That's a bad idea. Keep each potential team member in mind, and if they say they are too busy right now, then ask them, "Is it ok if I check back with you in a few months?" These are people you have prayed about, so don't let them go easily. Ask and keep asking.

In your follow-up ask, you might say something like, "Hey, I know I already talked to you about joining my team, but I haven't been able to get you off of my heart. I really think you would be great at this, and it's a powerful way to serve others. Can I ask if you might reconsider?" Every invitation is an affirmation, so affirm people often. Don't be afraid to invite someone to join your team multiple times.

INSPIRE

Scottish industrialist and philanthropist Andrew Carnegie said, *"If you want to be happy, set a goal that commands your thoughts, liberates your energy, and inspires your hopes."* Most people are not just interested in filling a need. People want to know how they can make a difference or how they will personally benefit from serving. In an online survey of 3,000 adults regarding volunteerism, 24% were looking for the work's impact, 23% wanted to learn or develop a new skill, and 15% were looking for a way to connect with others. This survey tells us there are more motivators for volunteers than merely filling a need. Let's look at these volunteer motivations individually.

For those who are looking for the impact that joining a prophetic team makes, don't just share your need for team members, share a testimony of how someone's life was deeply impacted by prophetic ministry. A great source to find testimonies and measurable results comes from the evaluation forms that we hand out at all prophetic appointments. Be ready to inspire others by arming yourself with powerful testimonies of prophetic ministry's impact.

Personal development is also a huge motivator for volunteering. People want to grow and master new skills. Every believer I have met wants to know the voice of God better. For those seeking personal development, you might share how prophesying over others has increased your own fellowship with Holy Spirit. You could also share how the prophetic community is regularly training in new ways to recognize and respond to the voice of God so that we are always increasing our prophetic skill. We practice prophecy beyond church ministry skill and into life skills such as business and personal consulting and even finding missing children. Prophetic skills help us tap into innovations, inventions, and creative solutions.

Being part of a team is an investment in your own life and development as a believer as well as blessing others.

Community and connection is another significant motivator for volunteers. Prophetic teams are a great place to connect with others of like heart and to feel a sense of community. Everyone loves to be a part of something greater than themselves. Many people are looking for a significant way to connect with other healthy people and to find their place within the Body of Christ. When someone joins your team, they are not just doing you a favor, you are meeting a very real need by giving them a place of significance, development, and connection. Do you see how an invitation should be more than the presentation of need? Great coaches are leaders who have learned to inspire those they invite.

CONNECT

For a coach, the connection can't end after the invitation. Once a team member invitation has been accepted, you need to get back with that person within 48 hours. It doesn't have to be much, just give them a quick call or invite them out for a coffee. Thank them for joining the team and lay out what the next steps are for being involved in the prophetic community. Ask them if they have any questions. Go over again the simple responsibilities of a team member. Make them aware of prophetic training opportunities like the Prophetic Company ACTIVATE events and online courses.[1] Over time, make sure that each team member knows the prophetic values and protocols. Also, let a team member know that you are available to them outside of prophetic ministry. Of course, you can set appropriate boundaries regarding your time and availability, but coaching is also extending the grace of pastoral care and connection to your team members' lives.

PRACTICE

There are several areas in which we train and practice. Our prophetic skills development is based upon my book *Basic Training in Prophetic Activation*. The *Basic Training* manual is a tool you can use and practice in a small group or family setting. Bethany Hicks' book *The God Connection* details the 12 receptors for spiritual information that Prophetic Company emphasizes. It, too, makes a great home group or personal training resource. Prophetic Company regularly hosts classes and seminars for basic training onsite and online. Upcoming training events are posted on the www. propheticcompany.com website and on social media.

In addition to these regular trainings, our teams do Facebook Live events where we invite the online community to prophesy with us over other attendees using the chat section. This is an exciting practice opportunity. Of course, there are many other resources for training and practice available as well. Be sure you are using a trusted source known for healthy prophetic interaction.

Find or create opportunities for your team members to exercise and grow their prophetic gifts. Make sure your team members feel equipped to stir up the gift of prophecy for their prophetic appointments by offering training opportunities in giving and receiving prophetic words.

These six steps: watch, pray, ask, inspire, connect, and practice should help you gain and keep the team members you need to operate as a strong part of the prophetic community. Never stop recruiting. If your team is full, then recruit for someone else's team. Always be watching among your team members for those who could serve as potential coaches. Coaches should reproduce themselves every one to three years. Producing coaches keeps the prophetic community healthy and growing together so we can serve more people. Every leader must know how to build and maintain a team. Recruiting is part of your leadership development as a coach.

CHAPTER 5
LEADING PEOPLE

"But everything should be done in a fitting and orderly way."

1 CORINTHIANS 14:39-40

N ow it's time to get down to the basics of what a prophetic team ministry appointment would look like and what your responsibilities as a coach would be within that meeting. For the purposes of this chapter, I am speaking of a prophetic ministry appointment within a church or conference event setting. The principles would be the same but the practices adjustable for ministry in other settings.

First of all, call your team members at least one week in advance of a prophetic ministry opportunity. A two-week notice or more is even better. Our local prophetic ministry leader publishes a listing of upcoming prophetic ministry opportunities every quarter.

Make sure you have at least two members available for your team. If you have extra members, you can rotate them through your team every half hour to an hour or have them substitute with another coach who might be lacking team members.

Ask your team members to arrive a minimum of fifteen minutes early to be in place when the call for prophetic ministry is given. Make sure team members have the specifics of where and when to meet. In our community, we have an administration team which manages assigning prophetic recipients to the ready and waiting ministry teams one at a time.

What should a prophetic team appointment look like? Here are six simple steps for the average prophetic ministry appointment.

WELCOME AND INTRODUCTIONS

When someone comes to your station for prophetic ministry, the coach should stand, welcome the person, and invite them to have a seat. Standing is a demonstration of respect and honor and shows the receiver who is in charge. Help guide the person to their seat before sitting down yourself. Ask the person's name and briefly introduce your team members. You can say something like, "This is Scott, Laura, and I'm Dan we are going to be encouraging you in the Lord today." Let them know that they can use their phone as a recording device and invite them to start the recording now. There isn't a lot of time for small talk, so move right to the next stage so you don't miss your opportunity to prophesy within the allotted time frame.

PRAY

Ask one of your team members to speak a quick prayer of blessing over the recipient. The brief prayer might go something like this, "Thank you, Father, that you have so many great things to say about (insert their name here). Open our eyes, our hearts, and our ears to the treasure of what You are speaking to them today." Your prayer should be super brief and set the tone for the appointment.

START

Immediately after the prayer, appoint someone to begin the ministry. Try not to have any awkward pause before the prophetic ministry time begins or uncomfortable pauses in-between ministry partners. If there is a long pause by one of the team members you can redirect by saying, "I can see you're seeking the Lord right now, lets come back to you in a minute." Then redirect to another team member or fill the space yourself. Our prophetic teams train to stir their gifts quickly and to develop continuity of flow among team members.

SHIFT

Take turns sharing. Don't allow any one person to dominate the prophetic appointment. Gauge your time as equally as you can among team members. If someone has a lot of content to share, then ask them to speak in short bursts of 1-2 minutes. After everyone has shared, the person with more can add additional content as time allows. Sometimes, it is helpful to work out non-verbal signals. If someone needs to pause, you can tap their knee or shoulder, or sometimes a head nod is sufficient. Work out some signals that keep the flow going for your team.

CLOSE

At the end of the ministry time, share a closing prayer, "Thank you, Father, for all the wonderful things you have spoken today. We release grace to process and activate these things in Jesus' name. Amen."

TRANSITION

At the end of the prayer, the coach should stand and thank the person for allowing you to share the Father's heart with them. Standing up lets the receiver know that your appointment has come to a close. If they start offering personal feedback, then kindly invite them to put that type of information on the evaluation form. If they have additional questions you can direct them to the prophetic leadership team or administrators. If the receiver keeps talking, then graciously share that you have another appointment coming. If you feel so led, you can arrange to meet them later for additional ministry or processing.[1]

Prophetic ministry time is never a place for counseling, sozo, deliverance, or healing. Our time is specifically crafted around what the Father is saying to this person. It can be tempting to go into an extended ministry time with someone in need, but other teams and times are already in place for this type of ministry. You can redirect a person in need to these types of opportunities. Coaches must keep the appointment focused around our primary purpose using the aforementioned six steps.

CHAPTER 6
COACHING PEOPLE

"Therefore encourage one another and build each other up, just as in fact you are doing."

1 THESSALONIANS 5:11

There is a good reason we call our team leaders "coaches." Coaching implies a different type of leadership. Sir John Henry Douglas Whitmore was a British race car driver and pioneer in the executive coaching industry who said, *"Coaching is unlocking people's potential to maximize their own performance. It is more often helping them to learn rather than teaching them."* I love the phrase, "helping them to learn rather than teaching." In keeping with the Prophetic Company ACTIVATE model of training, we believe coaching provides on-the-job learning opportunities in the prophetic field. Coaches facilitate an environment of discovery for improving how we all prophesy. Even in sports, a coach doesn't teach as much as suggest minor course corrections that improve overall performance. Following are a few things to watch for.

STRENGTHS

Coaches identify and encourage areas of strength. When a team member shares something powerful or accurate, affirm them in the moment with brief encouragement like, "Oh, great word" or, "So true." Practice verbalizing your praise. Don't just think it; say it. Create an atmosphere of affirmation that encourages risk. In this way, you build the faith of the whole team and make positive deposits into individual team members to balance any future withdrawals on the relationship when correction is necessary. Encouragement is the mother tongue of the Holy Spirit, and encouraging one another is one of our primary purposes for prophetic ministry. Learn to practice encouragement in the form of positive verbal feedback inside and outside of prophetic team ministry.

Coaches should also look for specialties. Does your team member often give accurate words of knowledge? Do they have a special ability in comforting people that manifests in tearful or joyful responses on the part of the receiver? Are their prophetic words rich with appropriate Scriptural content manifesting the breath of God on the living Word? Do you notice a special ability to craft language and metaphors to match their audience well?

Also, try to identify primary receptors. Would you say your member is primarily a seer, a hearer, a feeler, or a perceiver? You should be able to tell by the language they use and how they describe their prophetic impressions. A primary seer will often start a prophetic word with the phrase, "I see…" Primary hearers might say, "I'm hearing the Father say…" "I feel like…" might be the first phrase of a primary feeler. People with a primary knowing or perceiving perception may not use identifiers at the front of their phrase, but make direct statements of identity and destiny. Identifying potential spiritual strengths helps you know how to encourage, assign, and develop the skills of your team members.

Watch also for potential coaching skills in your team members. As you may remember, we ask every coach to recommend a new potential coach from their team members every one to three years. A coach should constantly be building and creating other leaders. Specifically watch for the same qualities identified in earlier chapters: prophetic skills, leadership skills, organizational skills, and, of course, character. Try to gently put team members in situations where these qualities are tested. Observe how they interact with other team members, how they treat the person receiving prophetic ministry, and how they exhibit restraint and follow protocols. Take the moments between appointments as another opportunity to do brief real-time affirmations. You might say something like, "Hey, I really appreciated how you yielded to your partner and made room for their word." Or, "Hey, thanks for honoring our time limits. I could see that you had a lot more to give, but I thought you did a great job of giving just the right amount." These kinds of verbal affirmations will encourage development while reinforcing structure and protocol.

DEVELOPMENT

A coach also speaks to potential areas of development both in real-time situations and outside of the prophetic appointments. If one of your team members is having trouble getting a word, the coach gently reminds them of some of our tools, "Are you seeing or sensing anything?" "Is a song or Scripture verse coming to mind for this person?" The coach can also ask direct questions like, "What weapon or tool do you believe best represents them?" Or, "What type of shoes do you believe fits this season for them?" Practice using leading questions like these that help team members stir up the gifts of God within them.

When a prophetic word is partial or vague, the coach helps team members go deeper by asking probing questions, "What do you think that means?" Or, "Can you describe that in a little more detail?" If your team member doesn't have an answer, you can help to bail them out with some additional content or an interpretation, but resist the urge to jump in until you have given them the opportunity to elaborate. Sometimes, all a team member needs is a little reminder or encouragement to go deeper. I often silently pray for the other members of the team while they are speaking.

If a team member is consistently getting stuck or not going very deep with their words, a coach can make arrangements to meet with the team member on a future occasion to do some activation exercises for developing their gifts.[1] If your team member is always starting a word with, "I see..." or "I hear...," then you might help them develop one of their other receptors to complement their primary way of receiving.

PERSONAL

A coach is also a life skill trainer. Pay attention to what your team members are going through in their personal life. Offer prayer, wisdom, and a listening ear when they need to process questions, are going through trials, or are facing major decisions. In the prophetic community, we are not only committed to developing the person's gifts but to also developing and loving the person. It's very important that we find ways to demonstrate a genuine interest in the person, not just their gifting.

If your team member is facing a situation that is beyond your ability to coach, refer them to a trusted professional or pastoral leader. Practice appropriate levels of confidentiality by asking permission before sharing anything spoken in private by your team member. If you are in an extreme situation where the person is in danger, breaking the law, or harming someone else then confidentiality does not apply. In any of those cases, give them twenty-four hours to seek verified help or let them know that you will be contacting appropriate authorities. Ultimately a healthy heart, home, marriage, and vocational environment will contribute to the quality of ministry a team member produces. Help to cultivate healthy team members.

CHAPTER 7
CONFRONTING PEOPLE

"A good objective of leadership is to help those who are doing poorly to do well and to help those who are doing well to do even better."

JIM ROHN

had a great dad, but he wasn't a natural confronter. He grew up with so much conflict in the home that he avoided confrontation whenever possible. This example gave me the impression that confrontation was a bad thing. Decades later, I heard the prophet Graham Cooke say, *"Confrontation is the primary tool for relational upgrades."* That was a new thought for me. By avoiding unpleasant conflict, I was forfeiting opportunities for relational upgrades.

Around the same time, I learned that a supernatural school north of us used a tool called "vision-based discipline." They believed that all negative performance was based upon a lack of vision because Scripture says, *"Where there is no revelation, people cast off restraint."* *(Proverbs 29:18)* From this principle, prophetic vision became a helpful key to my ability to confront. I began to understand that my own dread of conflict created an atmosphere of fear in the room. No matter how well I addressed an issue, the confrontation seldom went well because people could sense my fear and dread. Conversely, when I began to focus on the things that I love and appreciate about the person I was confronting and took time to dream about a better future for them, it created an atmosphere of faith and destiny where the confrontation went well. I would literally have people on numerous occasions shaking my hand and profusely thanking me for taking the time to sow into them after a confrontation. By intentionally using my prophetic grace to look for what people did well and where I saw them best fitting in the next three to five years, I began to see those upgrades that Graham Cooke spoke about.

This vision- and value-based confrontation gave a greater context of encouragement to the issue that I needed to address. It was more than an affirmation sandwich where you first say something positive, then layer on your confrontation topped with another affirming statement; it became the context for confrontation. I wasn't sandwiching correction between two contrived affirmations, I was genuinely appreciating and meditating on what was great about this person and where they were heading. Now, I am convinced that a poor performance in any situation is most often a vision or value issue.

Confrontation is important to coaching, and it doesn't need to be negative. Your attitude about conflict and correction will affect how well you confront and the atmosphere you create for the receiver. There are times when team members need to be confronted, but most of these are minor issues. Let's look at a few of the minor corrections that you can make in real-time during a prophetic appointment.

MINOR REAL-TIME CORRECTIONS

If as a coach you see a team member consistently taking too long, then tap them on the shoulder and use your worked-out hand signal or otherwise gently interrupt. You might say something like, "Excuse me for a minute, I'm going to break in here because our time is running short." This is a brief example of a minor real-time correction.

Another instance where you should gently interrupt is when you believe a team member is missing a prophetic word or using wrong, unbiblical, or inaccurate information. You might say something like, "I'd like to break in here for a minute to clarify something you said…" In that moment, you can turn the word by redirecting or fixing what was spoken incorrectly. Coaches do not let a team member continue in a wrong direction. Pay attention to how your team members respond to these types of disruptions and redirects. Make sure they aren't hurt or become hesitant through the interruption. Take a moment between appointments to give the person a coaching tip or some encouragement on how they could re-craft or approach their word to better fit our goals and values.

Words that are coming across too mystical, lofty, or outside of the team member's authority should also be steered in another direction. For instance, if someone is going deep into a vision, dream, or description they should be interrupted or reminded to move from the impression to what it means. If a person is outside of their authority by calling out five-fold gifts, correction, or inappropriate direction, then you will need to interrupt with a redirect. It is also appropriate to gently correct a team member when they are diverting from the primary purpose like moving into a time of healing, counseling, or deliverance, or if they begin to preach or teach. In these situations, remind your team that we are only here to give prophetic words and ministry. You can direct the receiver to a place where they can set up an appointment to receive these other types of ministry. Make sure you are serving a balanced diet of affirmations with only a seasoning of gentle correction. If someone is constantly off, then you need to set an appointment with them for a deeper journey into the issue.

ADDITIONAL MEETING CORRECTIONS

There are several situations where a correction or confrontation should occur outside of the real-time prophetic ministry environment. You should schedule to meet with that person in a timely way—usually within 48 hours is best. Confront before you forget the major details or get distracted with other things. Bringing up offenses that are old can give the impression that you withheld information or have been harboring negative feelings. Addressing issues close to when they occur is important for a culture of encouragement and healthy communication.

Arranging a discussion with a team member might be needed if you observe a team member consistently giving the same type of word to multiple people. Repetitive subjects may show an immaturity in skill, a favorite theme, or a fixation arising from a personal need. You will want to take a little time to get to the root of why this team member's prophetic words are so often sounding the same. Be prepared to accurately cite examples. Encourage the team member by mentioning things they are doing well. Let them know that you are there to help them grow and develop their prophetic gifting.

The following section offers some humorous personifications of the types of problems you are likely to face with team members and some brief coaching tips on what to say or do in response. These brief descriptions focus on some of the other problems that may require additional meeting confrontations.

> **Dark Dennis**—This is a person who may have good content but is often drawn to where a receiver is hurting or suffering. The result is their words may come off slightly dark, depressing, or

sad. Remind Dennis to speak to the treasure and encourage, strengthen, and comfort.

Dominant Doris—This is the team member who consistently uses five minutes of the seven-minute team time delivering their prophetic words. Remind Doris that we don't speak everything we receive. Leave room for others and work in a team. You can always jump back in later if there is a long pause or opportunity to share more.

Repetitive Ralph—This person shares the same word in different ways. They use multiple synonyms of the same word to lengthen their message and are overly descriptive of their own experiences. Remind Ralph of our value for "brief and amazing." Prophetic words don't have to be long to be deep.

Teacher Tina—This person shares a word and then explains and interprets what it means using Scripture and personal experiences. Remind Tina to let the word speak for itself and that prophetic appointments are not a pulpit nor are they to be processing time.

Super Word Sam—This person delivers over-the-top words to everyone promising cars, houses, new jobs, ministries, calling people to offices, etc. Remind Sam that we are accountable for the words we give and not to give any word that he would not be willing to process or walk through with that person over time. Don't over-promise.

Visionary Valerie—This person shares a long vision or impression but does not share what it means or what the actual word is. Remind Valerie to ask Holy Spirit, "What does this mean?" The impressions are not the word; they are simply how we perceive the prophetic information.

Authorizing Adam—This person constantly includes phrases like, "God says...God showed me...Thus saith the LORD..." Remind Adam that we know in part and prophesy in part. (1 Corinthians 13:9) It's better to say, "I feel like the Lord is saying..." "I believe the Lord is saying..." Because we hold such a strong value for judging and processing every prophetic word your language should leave room for input and testing.

Of course make sure you are practicing relational accounting—that is, don't make more "withdrawals" than "deposits" into your team members, or you will find your relational equity overdrawn. A team member might feel like the only time you talk to them is for the purpose of correction, and that doesn't feel good. Take time to notice things your team members are doing well and comment on them in real time outside of a confrontation situation. If a person only hears praise before a confrontation then they won't take the encouragement seriously. Make deposits of genuine praise and encouragement to build up your team. Healthy confrontation skills are important for any leader. Confronting prophecies or behavior in conflict with our values facilitates the building up of the entire community and presents an opportunity for a personal upgrade on the part of your team members.

CHAPTER 8
CALLING LEADERS

"Jesus went up on a mountainside and called to him those he wanted, and they came to him. He appointed twelve that they might be with him and that he might send them out to preach and to have authority to drive out demons."

MARK 3:13-15

Building prophetic teams is not just about performing a function, it is an act of aligning with the mission of Jesus Christ and impacting the world with leaders who know the voice of God. The leadership specialist John Maxwell says,

The single biggest way to impact an organization is to focus on leadership development. There is almost no limit to the potential of an organization that recruits good people, raises them up as leaders, and continually develops them.

Calling leaders up from ordinary people mirrors the method of Jesus for changing the world. Jesus invested Himself in a team of twelve for a few years, and that small group *"turned the world upside down." (Acts 17:6 NKJV)*

My spiritual mentor, Pastor Cleddie Keith, often said, "Nothing gives a man more dignity than to know that he can hear the voice of God." Practicing prophetic ministry restores dignity. Training and facilitating the gift of prophecy connects people to the voice of the Father who shaped the universe with His words. When our voices align with His voice, nothing is impossible. (John 15:7) Coaches in this way open the door to the impossible. At the end of the day, coaching a prophetic team is more than providing a service; it is equipping and sending out world-changers.

When you accept an invitation to coach a team, you become an integral part of this powerful prophetic community. Coaches are the life-blood of any prophetic community. Coaches make the difference between a prophetic ministry and a prophetic community. When you accept the position as a prophetic coach, you are building people not just filling a need.

I have been doing prophetic team building long enough to know that the people you serve will impact lives for years to come. As a coach, you have the opportunity to build real disciples. Your disciples will transform nations. I am calling you to join me in this life-changing mission of raising a generation of sons and daughters who can prophesy. (Joel 2:28) Together, let's redefine what the prophetic can look like in our generation by building healthy prophetic communities founded on love and guided by biblical protocols.

CHAPTER 9
COACHING RESOURCES

OVERVIEW OF PROPHETIC COACH RESPONSIBILITIES

Coaches are expected to:

- **Attend regularly scheduled coach meetings.**
- **Assemble their teams** for regular prophetic ministry on designated Sundays, at conferences, and other scheduled events.
- **Make contact with team members** at least once a month outside of class or prophetic ministry time.
- **Attend social functions** of the prophetic community whenever possible. These build relationships and deepen our sense of community.
- **Attend schools and conferences** that strengthen their prophetic gifts and insight whenever possible.
- **Attend and contribute regularly to a local church or house church.**

WHAT TO DO WHEN YOU FEEL YOU HAVE A PROPHETIC WORD FOR THE CONGREGATION DURING A PUBLIC SERVICE OR GATHERING

1. Self-Evaluate

Ask if this is primarily a word for you or is it truly for the congregation? Most of what we receive during a service is speaking to us or our own situation. Make sure you are not speaking a word over the whole that God is aiming at you.

2. Content

Is what you have to say encouraging, comforting, and strengthening? Also, a word that is highly directional should be written out and submitted to leadership to evaluate over time rather than blurted out in the service without any judging or processing.

3. Bring It To a Point Person

Usually, you would not shout out a prophetic word during the service unless the leader opens the opportunity for that type of congregational expression. In our community, we appoint a prophetic point person and place them on the front row of the venue. These are members of our prophetic core or key staff members.

Do not take your prophetic word or impressions directly to the speaker for that day. Allow the speaker to stay focused on what God is saying to them. Take your prophetic perceptions to a point person to be evaluated.

The point person will judge whether the word is right for that moment. (1 Corinthians 14:29)

These are responses you might receive from the point person:

No. The point person may feel it is not a word for the group at this time. It doesn't mean the word is wrong or you did something wrong; it just may be out of time or not in keeping with the flow of the current direction of the service.

Wait. The point person may ask you to hold the word and wait to see if the flow of the service creates an appropriate opportunity to share. Wait nearby for further direction, and if the service goes a different way, then return to your seat and engage with the direction the service has taken.

Test. The point person may ask you to share it with other team members or leaders for further evaluation. Sometimes they will ask you to share it with the morning speaker for their opinion. Be clear and brief.

Watch. The point person may step up and speak the word on your behalf. Sometimes a word is better received from a person in authority. We shouldn't care who gets the credit for the word, but rejoice that the Lord is speaking to us.

Go. The point person may ask you to share the

word publicly from the microphone. Be clear and
brief. Don't preach or go into a story or vision.
Share only what you shared with the point
person or leader.

4. Stay Humble

Humility and gentleness make up the yoke of Jesus.
(Matthew 11:29) If the leadership feels it is not the right
word or the right time, do not get a negative attitude.
Prophetic teams and persons are present first to serve
the church body. Pouting or storming off will
immediately demonstrate immaturity and confirm that
it was the right decision to not have you share the word.

It's quite possible that you have received a true word
from God that could have fit the moment, but the
leadership felt led a different way or time would not
allow going this direction. Stay open handed with what
you bring. Bring it as a sacrifice before the Lord that He
can do whatever He wants with. Stay teachable. Stay
humble.

Remember that your attitudes reflect your heart, and
they represent the larger prophetic community. Don't
do something that makes it hard for the rest of the team
or will later limit your own ability to be heard. The
right word needs the right time *and* the right heart.

SAMPLE BABY DEDICATION PROTOCOL

Why do we recommend offering prophetic ministry at a baby dedication?

The purpose of a baby dedication is to set apart a baby, a child, or children as holy unto God. Parents dedicate their children to the Lord and declare their trust in His keeping power. The families acknowledge they are stewards of the children and ask for wisdom to bring their children up in a loving relationship with God. When the baby Jesus was taken to the temple to be "consecrated to the Lord," God put the prophets Simeon and Anna there to speak to the family's future. (Luke 2:22-39) We see this as a prototype of God desiring to speak prophetically to a child's destiny and a family's future.

Prophetic Declaration

As a company of prophetic persons in a church embracing modern day prophecy, it is our great pleasure to look into the future with and through God's eyes at the life of a baby or child. We get prophetic insight about a child and then craft that revelation into a prophetic declaration and blessing over that precious life. The prophetic declarations can be written, spoken, or prayed as a blessing over the child.

Potential Content of the Declaration

Here are some ways you can formulate this prophetic content:

- Ask God to reveal His heart and give you the heart of a loving parent. What would prophecy look and feel like coming from such a loving, caring, affectionate voice speaking to the child as if they were your own?
- Look up the meaning of the baby's name and get a feel for what his or her name means and how God might be speaking through it.
- Research the meaning of the family name and watch for any inheritance gifts within that child. Does the child have any heritage from parental history which will be evident in their lives? (For example, do they walk in the same blessings, callings, or grace that a parent or great-great grandparent walked in?)
- Is there a biblical person who the child is called to resemble or share similar traits? Do they have the same personality or similar gifting as a specific biblical person?
- What are some of the angels assigned to their lives? How will these angels minister to and with the child? How can we declare their assistance and assignments into the life of this child?

The Baby Dedication Ceremony

1. An administrator will provide names in advance for the teams to pray over and prepare prophetic blessings.
2. At the time of the ceremony, church leadership invites the families to the front platform for the

public dedication.

3. At the close of the ceremony, the families are invited to meet the prophetic company in the back of the sanctuary for specific prophetic ministry over each child.

4. Teams of 3-4 persons per child should already be in place to welcome the families as they arrive.

5. The ministry team will take turns releasing prophetic words over the child and the family. Stay sensitive to the time, the reception of the family, and the behavior of the child. If the child is fussy, you can offer the parents the opportunity to be seated while you speak the words into a recording device and give them the recording later. We are primarily present to serve the families!

6. The prophetic coach can offer a closing prayer releasing grace over the prophetic words to be fulfilled in this child's life.

Written Prophetic Words

Though not a requirement, it is thoughtful to present your crafted prophetic words printed on a beautiful piece of paper (like parchment paper) rolled up as a scroll and tied around with a ribbon to the family on the day the baby is dedicated. This provides a beautiful written record for the family to accompany the certificate of dedication provided by the church.

SAMPLE CRITERIA FOR JUDGING PROPHETIC WORDS

Knowing how we judge prophetic words for accuracy helps you to shape the content of what you deliver. Let's examine some of the ways that prophetic words can be weighed carefully or judged:

- **Does it agree with Scripture?** No prophetic word will oppose or contradict what has been written in the Bible. You might not have a Scripture verse for everything that is prophesied, but a prophetic word will never be contrary to the written Word. If it takes someone away from the written word of God, it is not a true prophetic word.
- **Is it consistent with the character and nature of God?** In other words, can you see God saying this? Does it match His character traits as revealed in Scripture and His dealings throughout history? Does it make God look like God? Prophecy is what God is thinking and saying about you. He is a good God who says good and loving things about His children.
- **Is the word encouraging, comforting, and strengthening?** Scripture reveals that this is the primary purpose of New Testament prophecy. (1 Corinthians 14:3) If you have trouble discerning whether it matches this criteria, ask yourself if it would be considered a good word if it was spoken over one of your friends or family members.

- **Does it glorify God?** Would the journey and fulfillment of this promise draw you closer to God? Any word or its fulfillment should increase your friendship and fellowship with God. Beware of something that would take you in an opposite direction.

- **Does it resonate with you?** Do you feel the word is true even if parts of it are challenging? Is the word taking you in a direction that is counter to your will, or does it release a sense of peace, hope, or joy? Usually a prophetic word in its season will *agree* with or ignite something confirming within our hearts.

- **Does the word line up with gifts, graces, and callings that the Lord has given you?** Even though we can find a word challenging, it usually matches something God has already placed or prepared in our lives.

- **Do you trust the source?** Does the person giving the word have any reason to control or manipulate you? Would the person delivering the word receive any personal benefit from your following this prophetic word? Most abuse of prophecy in the past came from people manipulating and controlling others or even well-wishing for others —neither of which would result in an accurate prophetic word.

- **How do family, friends, and leaders who love you feel about the word?** Remember that judging prophecy should never be a private exercise. (1 Corinthians 14:29) Never contradict the interpretation of loved ones and leaders unless you are absolutely sure and ready to receive the full consequences of rejecting godly counsel. If you think your family members or local leaders are hearing incorrectly, you might want to check the word with other leaders or friends who you trust and who have demonstrated wise and accurate counsel in the past.

15 PROPHETIC QUESTIONS YOU CAN ASK TO DEEPEN YOUR PROPHETIC CONTENT

This is a list of questions you can ask the Father as you are listening for the prophetic word for the person you are speaking to. Obviously, you won't be able to ask all the questions in a single appointment; they are meant as "discussion starters" to kick off your word.

1. Father, how do you see this person?
2. Lord, what do you love about this person?
3. What does this person love? What are their passions, dreams, and imaginations?
4. What is this person concerned about? What are their burdens regarding places, people, or situations? (This question is related to the ministry of comfort.)
5. Where does this person fit? Who is their tribe? Who are their people?
6. What is in the Father's heart for this person? What are some of the promises the Father wants to make or affirm towards them?
7. Who is this person thinking about? Who is the person that is most on their mind?
8. What season of life is this person in? What is an appropriate promise or step of faith in this season?
9. What metaphor might best describe this person? What weapon or tool does the Father compare them to and why?
10. Who does this person remind you of? God loves comparing us to one of our heroes or to a

person of influence. This comparison can help speak to our course.

11. Where is this person going or has been that the Lord's blessing is upon?

12. Where is this person strong? It's fun to speak to someone's graces, gifts, and character strengths. It's another way the Father celebrates us.

13. What should this person be watching in hope for? Is there a past promise the Lord wants to confirm or upgrade?

14. What should this person watch out for or be concerned about? What are the obstacles to their potential success?

15. What key connections does this person have or are coming?

SAMPLE PROPHETIC MINISTRY FEEDBACK FORM

Feedback and input regarding your experience with our prophetic ministry teams is important to us. Thank you for taking a moment to give some feedback. This completed form can be returned to the box marked "Prophetic Feedback" on the info table in the lobby. You are not required to give your name.

Scripture tells us that you have the power to test and judge what was spoken over you.

> 1 Thessalonians 5:19-21—*Do not quench The Spirit; do not despise prophetic utterances; examine everything carefully, hold fast to that which is good.*

> 1 Corinthians 14:3—*But the one who prophesies speaks to men for edification, exhortation and consolation.*

Your Name _____

Today's Date _____

Names of ministry team members _____

_____

Prior to this, have you received prophetic ministry either here or at another church? ☐ Yes ☐ No

Were you able to clearly hear the team members who ministered to you today? ☐ Yes ☐ No

Did the prophetic ministry encourage you? ☐ Yes ☐ No

If yes, in what way? If no, what was not helpful or encouraging?

_____

_____

If the word spoken was of present or past things in your life, were these things accurate? ☐ Yes ☐ No

Describe

_____

_____

How would you rate your overall experience with the prophetic ministry teams? ☐ Positive ☐ Not Positive

Explain

_____

_____

Is there any way you feel the prophetic ministry could be improved? ☐ Yes ☐ No

Explain

_____

_____

If you have questions or concerns about anything that was said or done in your prophetic appointment and would like to be contacted, please share your contact information here:

Phone: _____

Email:_____

ADDITIONAL TRAINING OPPORTUNITIES FOR COACHES AND THEIR MEMBERS

Prophetic Company offers multiple online prophetic training courses at *PropheticCompanyAcademy.com*, including:

ACTIVATE PROPHECY 101: Ways To Hear

This ACTIVATE Course provides the first building block for establishing you in the gift of prophecy. You will discover multiple ways to receive prophetic information and grow confident in your ability to hear the voice of God.

31 Lessons

ACTIVATE PROPHECY 102: Ways To Deliver

This ACTIVATE course lays the next building block for advancing your ability to share a prophetic word. You will explore several ways to deliver a prophetic word and continue to increase the depth of your prophetic content and confidence.

31 Lessons

ACTIVATE PROPHECY 103: Ways To Grow

This ACTIVATE course continues your prophetic training by focusing on deepening your prophetic content, expanding your prophetic capacity, growing in continuity, and exploring prophetic counsel. We recommend taking Prophecy 101 & 102 beforehand.

32 Lessons

THE GOOD FIGHT: Prophetic Processing Course

In this interactive e-course, you will learn how to activate, mobilize, and accelerate the prophetic promises over your life so that by them you can fight the of faith. (1 Timothy 1:18)
58 lessons

NOTES

3. PROTECTING PEOPLE

1. McCollam, Dan. *Love and Prophecy*, Prophetic Company, Round Rock, Texas, 2019.
2. McCollam, Dan. https://www.propheticcompanyacademy.com/courses/living-on-the-right-side-of-the-cross-seminar.

4. RECRUITING MEMBERS

1. Visit www.propheticcompanyacademy.com.

5. LEADING PEOPLE

1. A great follow up tool is the book *The Good Fight: Prophetic Processing Manual* by Dan McCollam.

6. COACHING PEOPLE

1. *Basic Training for Prophetic Activation* by Dan McCollam contains dozens of practice exercises for boosting confidence and diversifying strengths.

ABOUT THE AUTHOR

Dan McCollam travels internationally as a prophetic speaker and trainer. In addition to having cultivated a vibrant prophetic community at his home church, Dan is co-founder of the Bethel School of the Prophets and Prophetic Company, Inc. Dan has published multiple resources on the prophetic and on worship, most of which you can find at Amazon.com or propheticcompany.com. Through Prophetic Company, Dan offers multiple levels of personal training for growing your ability to hear God and help others do the same.

Made in the USA
Columbia, SC
23 February 2024

31926748R00052